MY FAVORITE SOLO ALBUM

54 Pieces in
the Earlier Grades for Piano

Revised and Edited by
MAXWELL ECKSTEIN

CARL FISCHER®
62 Cooper Square, New York, NY 10003

0 8258 0154 0

O3223

ALPHABETICAL INDEX OF TITLES

Cover photograph courtesy of Steinway & Sons.

CONTENTS

China Doll

MAXWELL ECKSTEIN

mf a tempo
p
mf
p
mf
p
mf
p
p
pp

Minuet in G Major

J. S. BACH
(1685-1750)

Allegretto

Soldiers' March

Album for the Young

R. SCHUMANN, Op. 68, No. 2
(1810-1856)

03223

Taps

Campfire Revery

LOIS von HAUPT

This piece will remind you of the joy of summer time, scouting and camping with your friends and comrades. It will bring to mind the quiet of evening at camp, the sound of the bugle with its distant echo, and the "good-night song" of all the children.

* * *

Before beginning to practice and play this piece, *remember* that it is written in the key of G major (one sharp, F). It is in common or four-four time, meaning that there are four counts to a measure and every quarter note receives *one* count; a half note receives *two*, and a whole note *four* counts. You must also become acquainted with, and memorize the Italian words and their abbreviations, as explained at the foot of the page.

You must also pay attention to the left hand, which carries the dreamy melody, referred to as the "good-nigh' song" wherever it occurs.

*) *mf* abbreviation for Italian words *mezzo forte*, meaning *half-loud.*
**) *f* abbreviation for Italian word *forte*, meaning *loud, strong.*
***) *8va* abbreviation for Italian word *ottava*, meaning to play the notes thus marked *one octave* higher.
****) *pp* abbreviation for Italian word *pianissimo*, meaning *very softly.*
*****) *p* abbreviation for Italian word *piano*, meaning *softly.*

8va
(Die away)
8va
mf
p *****)
pp
A "good-night" song
Echo
8va
pp
simile
8va
(The Bugle)
8va
8va
8va
softer
(Die away)
8va
mf
p
pp

The Dancer
Valse Petite

MAXIM LITTOFF

This number is written in the key of F major, which has one flat, B in the signature. It is in three-quarter time, meaning three counts to each measure; each quarter note receives *one* count, each half note *two*, a dotted half note *three*, and an eighth note receives a *half* count.

In the first half of the number emphasize the left-hand melody—the right hand serving as the accompaniment. In the second half observe carefully the crossing of hands and sustain the dotted half notes in this section for their full value.

Explanation of signs and abbreviations:

(1)	*p*	Italian word *piano*, softly.
(2)	*Fine*	The end.
(3)	*mf*	Italian words *mezzo forte*, moderately loud.
(4)	*L. H.*	Left hand.
(5)	*R. H.*	Right hand.
(6)	*cresc.*	Italian word *crescendo*, gradually getting louder.
(7)	*rit.*	Italian word *ritardando*, getting slower.
(8)	*D. C.*	Italian words *Da Capo*, meaning to go back to the beginning and end at *Fine*.

(2) Fine
(4) L. H.
(3) mf
(5) R. H.
L. H.
R. H.
L. H.
p
R. H.
L. H.
R. H.
L. H.
(6) cresc.
R. H.
L. H.
R. H.
L. H.
R. H.
L. H.
mf
R. H.
(7) rit.

(8) D. C.

The Marines' Hymn

From the Halls of Montezuma

1. From the halls of Montezuma
To the shores of Tripoli,
We fight our country's battles
On the land as on the sea;
First to fight for right and freedom
And to keep our honor clean;
We are proud to claim the title
Of United States Marine.

2. Our flag's unfurled to every breeze
From dawn to setting sun,
We have fought in every clime or place
Where we could take a gun;
In the snow of far off northern lands,
And in sunny tropic scenes,
You will find us always on the job,
The United States Marines.

3. Here's health to you and to our corps
Which we are proud to serve;
In many a strife we've fought for life,
And never lost our nerve.
If the Army and the Navy
Ever gaze on Heaven's scenes,
They will find the streets guarded by
The United States Marines.

Official Song of the United States Marine Corps
Arranged and Edited by Maxwell Eckstein

O3223

The Cellist

VIRGINIA WINES SCOVILL

The title of this piece will remind you of the player of one of the most beautiful of all string instruments. It has four strings, the two lower ones sounding very deep and full, and the two higher ones sweet and expressive. Long sustained melodies sound particularly beautiful on this instrument and the music is written just like that for your left hand, in the *bass clef.* In this piece your left hand should imitate the cellist as he plays an expressive waltz melody on his instrument. You should try to connect the notes smoothly and evenly, just as he would do with his bow.

* * * * *

Before beginning to practice and play this piece, *remember* that it is written in the key of C major, furthermore, that it is written in three-four (3/4) time, meaning that there are three counts to a measure, and that every quarter note receives *one*, every half note *two* and every dotted half note *three* counts.

The piece should be played in moderate, rather dreamy tempo and the left-hand melody should stand out prominently and with swinging rhythm. The right-hand chords should be practiced carefully and should all be played rather softly so as not to interfere with the swing of the left-hand melody.

From to , known as the middle section, the tempo should be slightly animated and the right-hand melody should stand out just as prominently as the left-hand melody did at first. After this the left hand should take up the melody again, just as it did at the start.

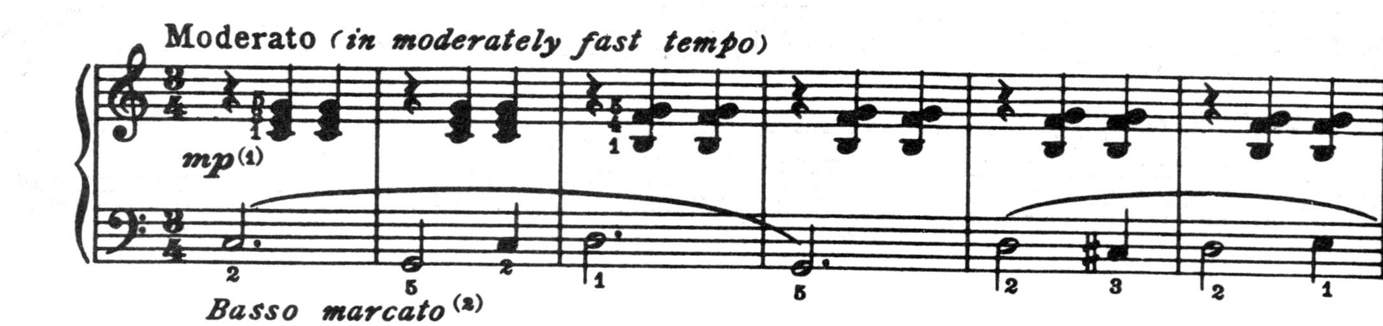

(1) *mp* abbreviation for Italian words *mezzo piano*, meaning *half soft.*
(2) *Basso marcato* Italian words meaning that the bass (left-hand) melody should be *marked* or played with emphasis.
(3) *Ritard* abbreviation for Italian word *ritardando*, meaning getting slower and slower.
(4) *a tempo animato* Italian words meaning *a tempo*, at the original tempo;
animato animated, meaning in this case, to pick up the tempo as at first but slightly quicker.
(5) *a tempo primo* Italian words meaning the tempo exactly as at first.

03223

a
ritard.(3)
a tempo animato(4)
b
ritard.
a tempo primo(5)

Swinging Lanterns

A Chinese Dance

MAXWELL ECKSTEIN

Shut your eyes and imagine that you are on a magic carpet, being carried over the seas to the far-off land of China. Now look down quickly and see the bright lights below you; let us stop off here and watch the Dance of the Swinging Lanterns. Here come the little almond-eyed boys and girls and the dance begins. How graceful they look, their little feet going pitter-patter ever so lightly, and each one swinging his lantern to and fro in perfect time with the music. One by one, the lanterns go out, the dance comes to an end, and little Chinese boys and girls hurry home to bed.

* * *

Before beginning to practice and play this piece, *remember* that it is written in the key of E minor, relative to G major. Every F is played F sharp.

The time is four-four (4/4), so there are four counts to each measure. Each quarter note receives *one* count, each half note *two* counts, and each eighth note a *half* count.

Notice that some notes have a dot placed over them. This means that the note is to be played short or detached. The name given to this is *staccato*, an Italian word meaning short.

Be careful to keep the right hand very relaxed and quiet during the playing of the piece.

Explanation of signs and abbreviations:

1)	*p*	*Piano*, meaning softly.
2)	*leggiero*	Lightly.
3)	>	A note marked with this sign receives an additional accent.
4)	*mf*	*Mezzo-forte*, meaning half loud.
5)	(decrescendo hairpin)	Same as *decrescendo*, meaning to decrease in loudness.
6)	*poco ritard*	Ritard a little.
7)	*dim.*	*Diminuendo*, meaning diminish in loudness.
8)	𝄐	*Fermata*, or a pause, which means that the note is held a little longer than ordinarily.
9)	*pp*	*Pianissimo*, meaning very softly.

O3223

The Little Navajo

Indian Intermezzo

MAXIM LITTOFF

This little piece, both in music and words, illustrates how the young Navajo Indian boys play and dance in their hours of recreation. Like their elders they tell you how brave and bold they are, and how they will go on the war path in search of their foes; the song ends with the customary war dance accompanied by the beating of the *tom-tom*, a little drum used by the Indians on all occasions.

* * *

Before beginning to practice and play this piece, *remember* that it is written in the key of A minor and that it is in four-four (or common) time. Furthermore, be sure to pay attention to the time value of the notes, remembering that whole notes receive *four*, half notes *two*, and dotted half notes *three* counts, while quarter notes, and each group of two eighth notes receive *one* count.

The piece should be played with animation, strict precision as to time, and the rhythm should be further emphasized by observing those notes in the left hand with accent marks (>).

see the foe, Lit - tle
Nav - a - jo?
The War Dance (Faster)
(loud)
(softer)

2-6-96

Little Menuet in G

L. van BEETHOVEN
(1770-1827)

O3223

Trio

Men. D. C.

Jean and Babette

French Playtime Folk Songs

MAXWELL ECKSTEIN

This piece is made up of two songs dear to the hearts of French children. The first one, *J'ai du bon tabac*, means "I've some good tobacco," but when they play, the children tease each other by singing; "I've some bon-bons in my bag, but not one for you."

The second song, *A Paris*, means "To Paris let's go." In playing this the French children make believe they are on a hobby horse and are on imaginary visits to far distant places:

To Paris, to Paris, to Paris,
Then come home again.
To Rouen, to Rouen, to Rouen,
Then come home again, etc.

* * *

Before beginning to practice and play this piece, *remember* that it is written in the key of C major (no sharps or flats). It is in common or four-four time, meaning that there are four counts to a measure and every quarter note receives *one* count; two eighth notes get *one* count and a half note receives *two* counts.

The melodies, as you will notice, are formed on the five finger position from start to finish.

*)	*p*	abbreviation for Italian word *piano*, meaning *softly*.
**)	*f*	abbreviation for Italian word *forte*, meaning *loud, strong*.
***)	*poco rit.*	abbreviation for Italian words *poco ritardando*, meaning *somewhat slower*.

f **)
p
À Paris (To Paris let's go)
poco rit. ***)

Minuet No. 1, with Trio

W. A. MOZART
(1756-1791)

This Minuet and Trio were composed by Mozart in 1761, at the age of five.

Allegro

JOS. HAYDN
(1732-1809)

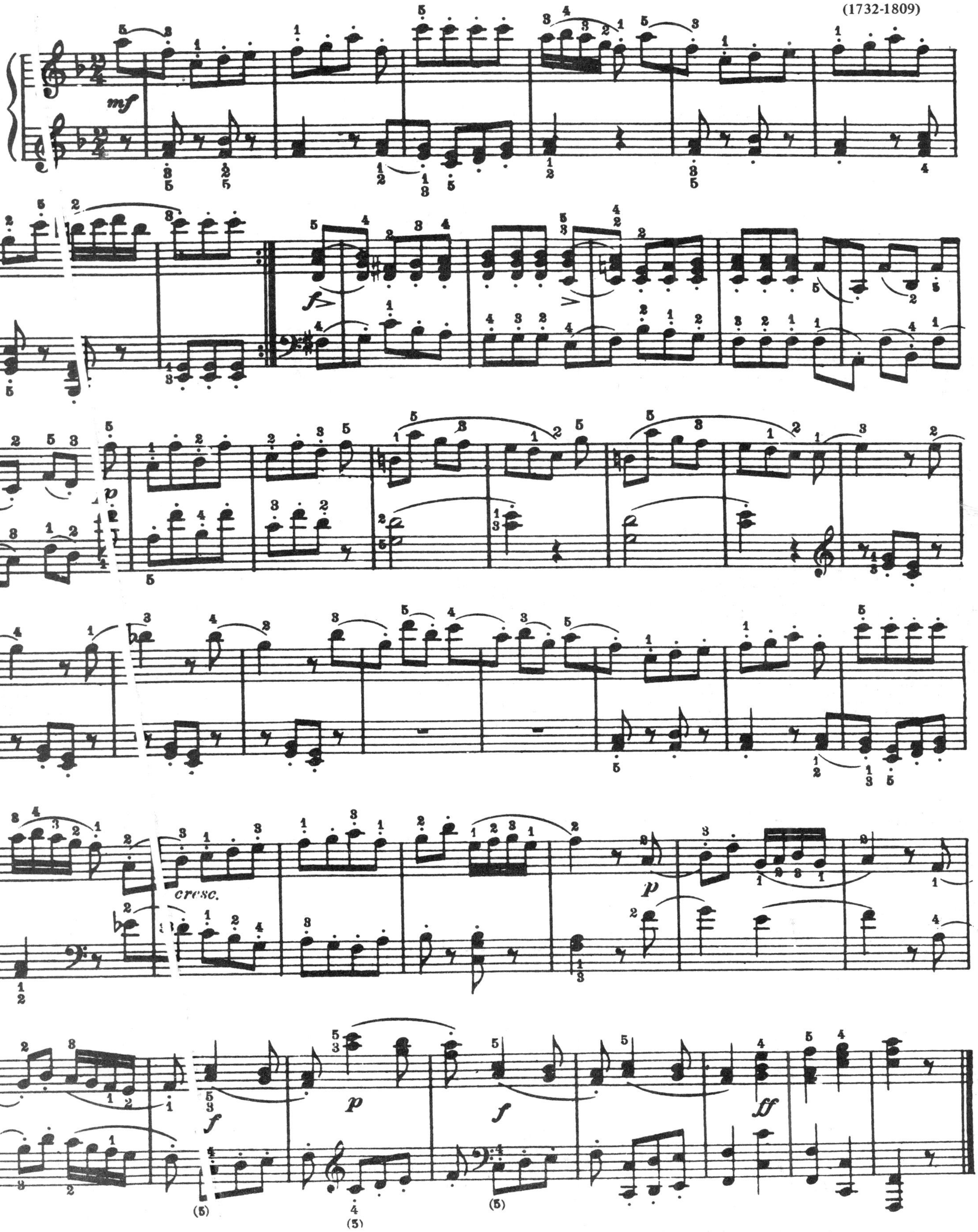

Country Gardens

Handkerchief Dance

cresc.

Turkey in the Straw

American Folk Tune
Arranged by Maxwell Eckstein

p
cresc.
f
mf
f

Serenade

Softly through the night is calling,
Love, my song to thee.
Shades of night are swiftly falling,
Dearest, come to me!

In the moonlight gently swaying,
Whisp'ring leaves I hear;
"No one listens," they are saying,
"Fair one, do not fear."

(English version by Alice Mattullath)

FRANZ SCHUBERT (1797-1828)
Arranged by Maxwell Eckstein

Andante moderato

p espressivo

pp

Ped. simile

p

pp

mf

03223

p
mf
p
dim.
rit. e dim.
pp

Tales from the Vienna Woods

Waltz

JOHANN STRAUSS, Jr. (1825-1899)
Arranged by Maxwell Eckstein

Fine
D. S. al Fine

Unfinished Symphony

Theme

FRANZ SCHUBERT (1797-1828)
Arranged by Maxwell Eckstein

p
p
f
p
dim.
pp

3-12-96

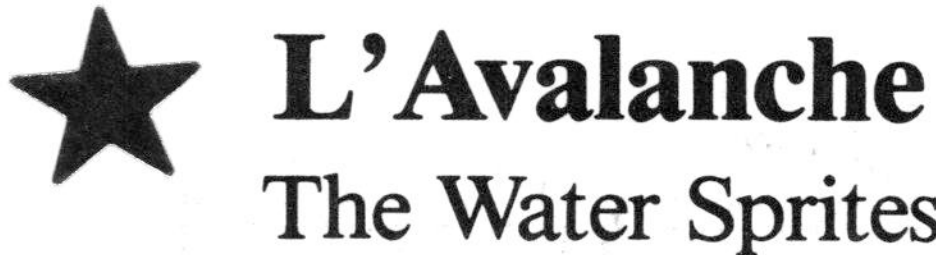

★ L'Avalanche
The Water Sprites

STEPHEN HELLER, Op. 45, No. 2
(1815-1888)

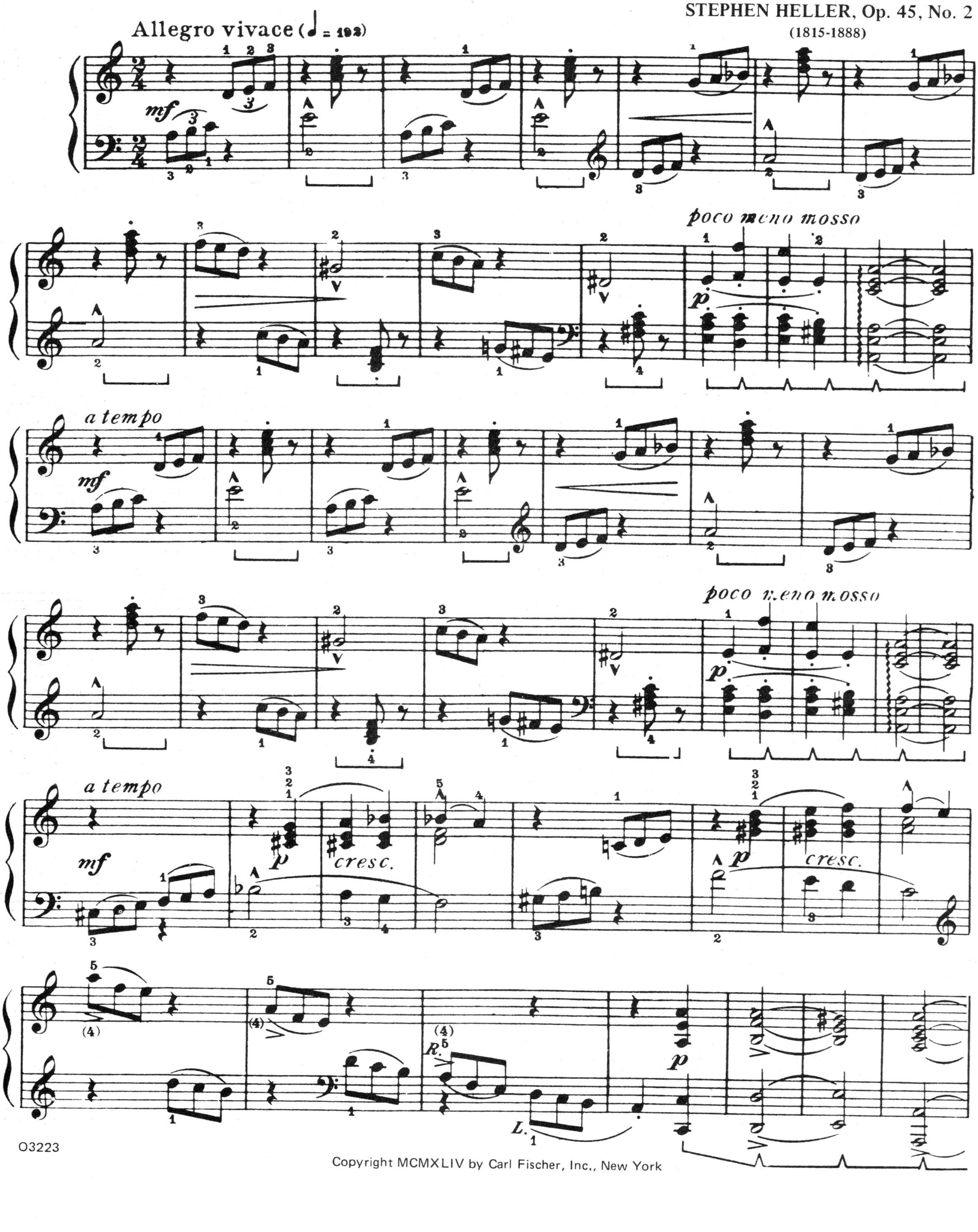

Allegro vivace (♩ = 192)
mf
poco meno mosso
p
a tempo
mf
poco meno mosso
p
a tempo
mf
p
cresc.
p
cresc.
p

O3223

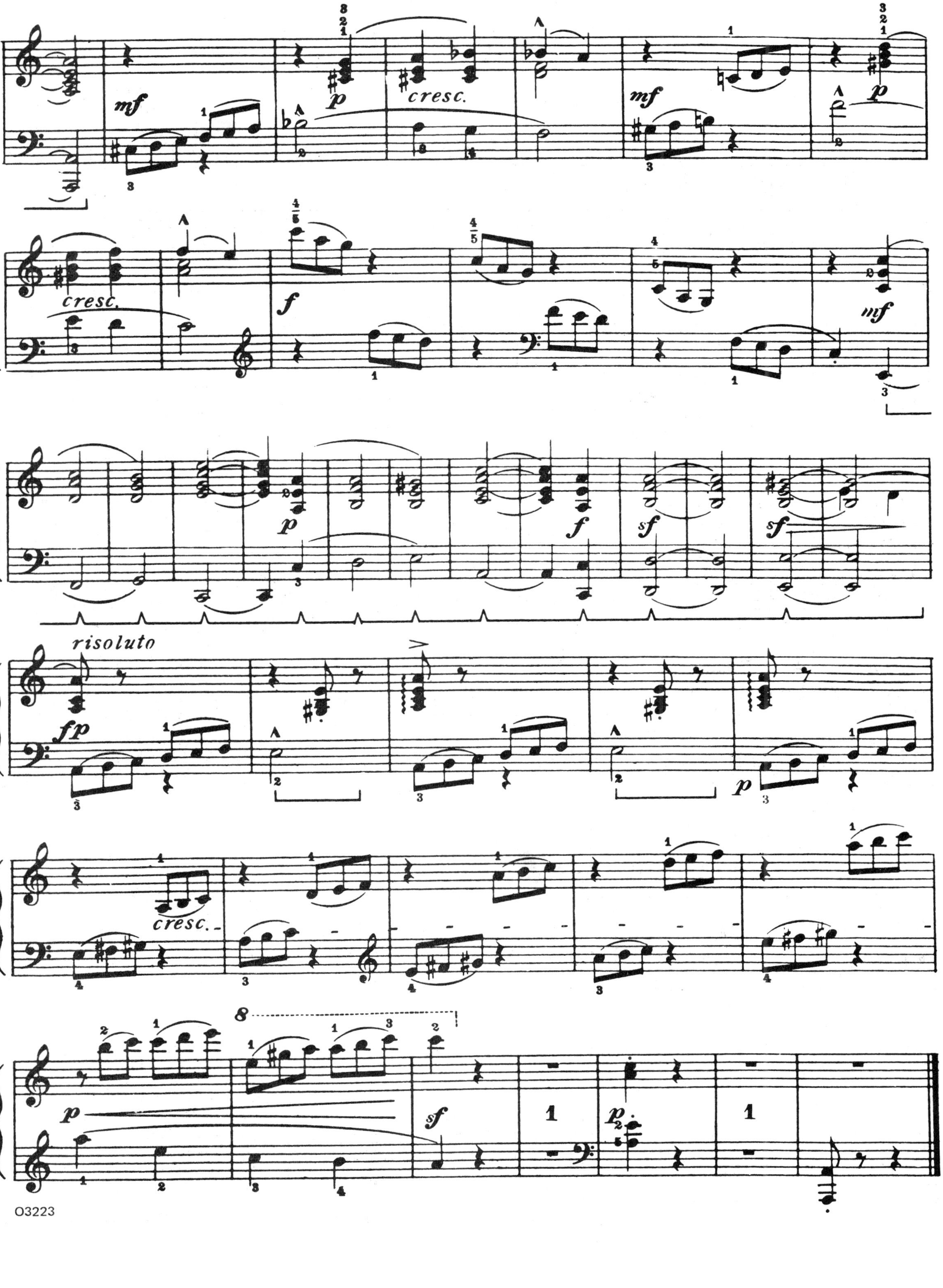

cresc.

cresc.

risoluto

cresc.

Spinning Song

A. ELLMENREICH, Op. 14
(1816-1905)

cresc.
p
cresc.
p
legg.
cre - scen - do.
f
p cre - scen -
do.
poco rit.
a tempo
p
rit.

3-19-96

Knight Rupert

Album for the Young

R. SCHUMANN, Op. 68, No. 12
(1810-1856)

cresc.
p
sf
p
sempre legato
fp
f
f f f
ff

Sonatina
in G Major

L. van BEETHOVEN
(1770-1827)

Romanze.

mf

cresc

f *dim.* *e rit.* *a tempo*

p

Voice of the Heart

Romance sans paroles

HENRI VAN GAEL, Op. 51

O3223

rall.
p a tempo.
f

f
dim.
rall.
p a tempo

legato
p
morendo.
pp

8/27/96

Gertrude's Dream Waltz

L. van BEETHOVEN
(1770-1827)

Andante con espress.

p

cresc.

ff

dolce
(a)
1.
2.
1.
2.
p
poco rit.
(a)

5-7-96

On the Beautiful Blue Danube

Waltz

JOH. STRAUSS (1825-1899)
arr. by L. Streabbog, Op. 86

cresc.

CODA.
Fine.

2-20-96

Tarentelle

PAUL BEAUMONT

p legg.

p

p
p

f
ff
l.h.
r.h.
Prestissimo.
ff

8\13\96

Rustic Dance

C. R. HOWELL

sf
rit.
f a tempo
p

Tempo Imo

cresc.
sf
rit.
a tempo
ff accel.

6/4/96

★Für Elise
Albumblatt

(Composed 1808)
L. van BEETHOVEN
(1770-1827)

dolce
p con espressione
cresc.
dim.
p
p
dim. e poco rit. pp
a tempo

mf
dimin.
p
dim.
pp
meno mosso
p
cresc.
f
dim.
p
cresc.
f
dim e rit.

8va
8va
leggiero
pp rall.
Tempo I
mf
dim.
p
pp
mancando

5\21\96

The Happy Farmer

Album for the Young

R. SCHUMANN, Op. 68, No. 10
(1810-1856)

O3223

Tulip

Allegretto

HEINRICH LICHNER, Op. 111, No. 4
(1829-1898)

p
f
p
rit.
p espressione
a tempo
pp
p
pp
mf
pp
p
mf

p
p orillante
f
ff
sf

6\12\96

The Wild Horseman

Album for the Young

R. SCHUMANN, Op. 68, No. 8
(1810-1856)

The Music Box

ED. POLDINI
(1869-1906)

mf
p
mf
f
diminuendo
8
sf brillante

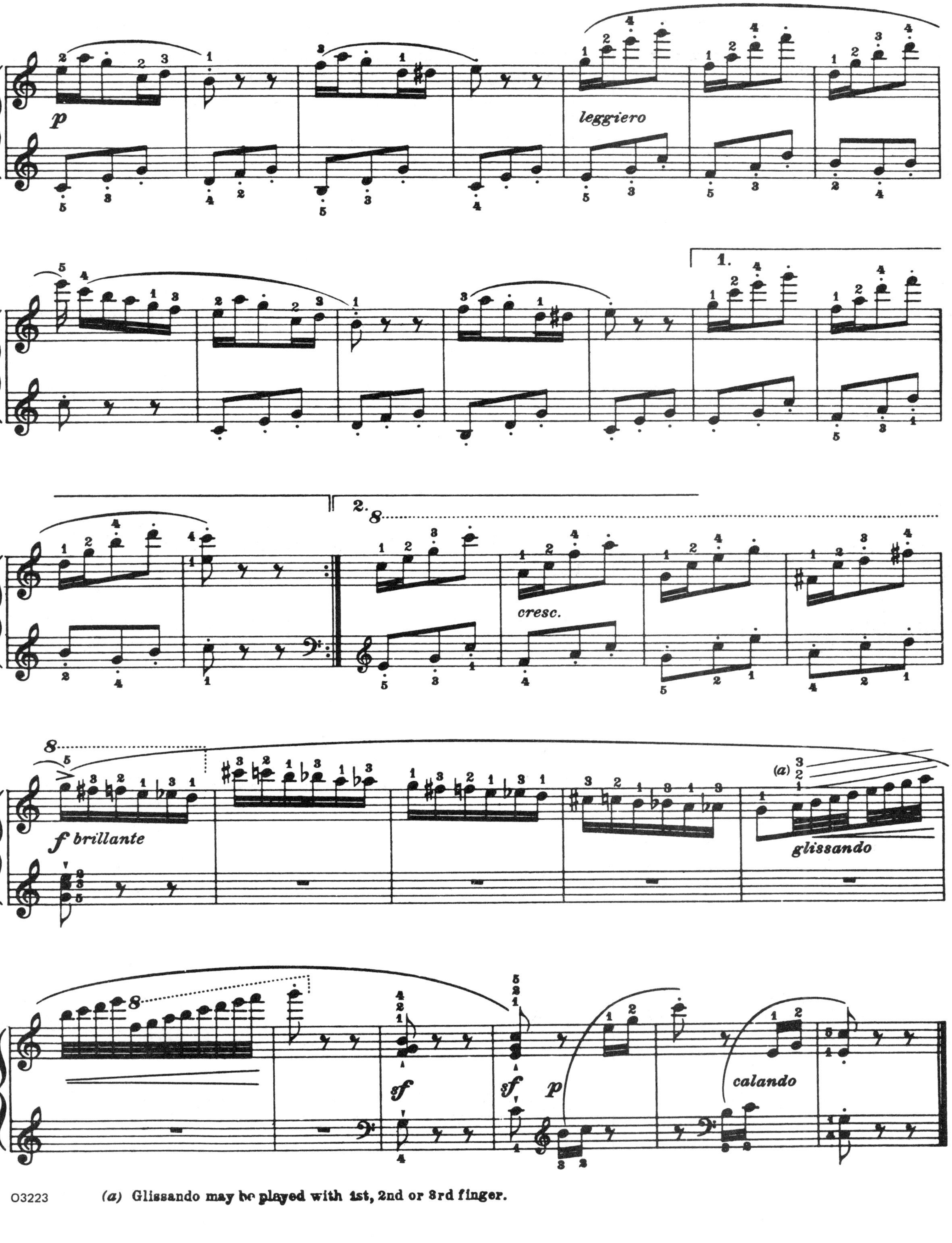
p
leggiero
1.
2.
cresc.
f brillante
(a)
glissando
sf
sf
p
calando

(a) Glissando may be played with 1st, 2nd or 3rd finger.

Butterflies

W. LEGE, Op. 59, No. 2

Vivace.

8va

mf

8va

p

p

pp

cresc.

8va
mf
Pedale come primo.
dolce calmato.
p
con Ped.
legato il basso.
p

8va
p
con Pedale.
mf
sempre dim.

In the Meadow

HEINRICH LICHNER, Op. 95
(1829-1898)

senza rit.
p leggiero.
p con espressione.
rit.
a tempo.
cresc.
f
p
rit.
espress.
p
a tempo.
ten.
ritard.
ten.

a tempo.
ten.
ten.
8va
p leggiero.
con fuoco.
8va
8va
p rit - ard - an - do.
a tempo.

The Fountain

C. BÖHM
(1844-1920)

(a) *For small hands* – play lower note of the octave a this and subsequent measures.

il canto marcato

R.H.

Tempo I

p

f

f

f

p
mf
cresc.
f

Venetian Boat Song No. 2

Song without Words

F. MENDELSSOHN, Op. 30, No. 6
(1809-1847)

f
ff
sf
dimin.
tr
pp
sf
dimin
p
p
cresc.
al
f
dim.
p
cresc.
al
f
sf
dim.
p
sf
dim.
pp

Solfeggietto

CARL PHILLIPP EMANUEL BACH
(1714-1788)

Non troppo vivo

sopra

a) ossia:

O3223

Consolation

Song without Words

F. MENDELSSOHN, Op. 30, No. 3
(1809-1847)

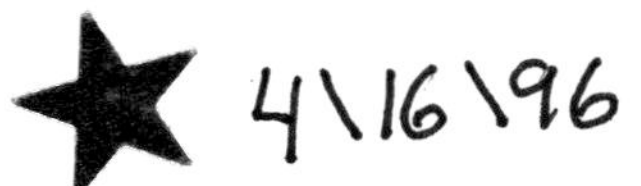

The Gypsies' Camp

FR. BEHR, Op. 424, No. 3
(1837-1898)

Allegretto con moto

f *marcato*

riten. un poco

a tempo

pp *leggiero*

il basso sempre staccato

mf

f

p
mf
f
marcato

a tempo
riten. un poco
pp
stacc.
mf
f

p *grazioso*

mf

p

f

un poco più lento

p

riten. un poco

a tempo

pp

stacc.

O3223

Scarf Dance

Air de Ballet

C. CHAMINADE
(1857-1944)

p delicatamente.

p dim.

pp

cresc.

f

dim.

p

pp rubato.

cresc.

f

dim.

p

pp

8va

p delicatamente.
dim.
pp
cresc.
f
dim.
pp rubato.
cresc.
f
dim.
p
pp rit.
f sec.

Sonatina

M. CLEMENTI, Op. 36, No. 1
(1752-1832)

Andante
dolce
legato
cresc.
ten.
dolce
poco cresc
dim.
Vivace
or easier
or easier

dim.

Gold and Silver

Valse

FRANZ LEHAR
(1870-1948)

Tempo di Valse (Moderato)

p

con pedale

mf

p

f

p

f

p
mf
f
fz

Dorothy

Old English Dance

SEYMOUR SMITH

f
cresc.
ff
ff
mf
ff
mf
pp legatissimo.

ff
mf
f
mf
sf
mp

R. H.
f
mp
R. H.
f
ff
mf
f
f
cresc. molto.
ff
sf
mp dolce e meno mosso.
a tempo.
ff

Le Coucou

Rondeau

CLAUDE DAQUIN
(1694-1772)

03223

a)
p
cre
scen
do
tr
mf
b)
p legg.
cre
scen
do
dim.
p legg.
a) easier:
b)

cre - scen - do

dim.

p

poco - a - poco - cre - scen - do

mf e sempre

cre - scen - do

f

a)

mf

a): 

cre - scen - - do
poco rit.
a tempo
p e leggiero
cre - - scen - do
dim.
pp legg.
poco cre - scen - do
dim. e rit.
pp

6\18\96

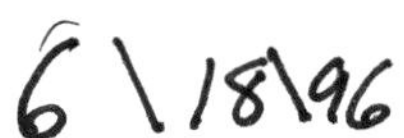

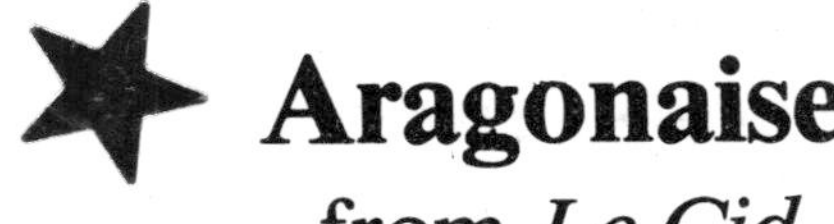

★ Aragonaise
from *Le Cid*

JULES MASSENET
(1842-1912)

Allegro brillante (♩.=72 M.M.)

O3223

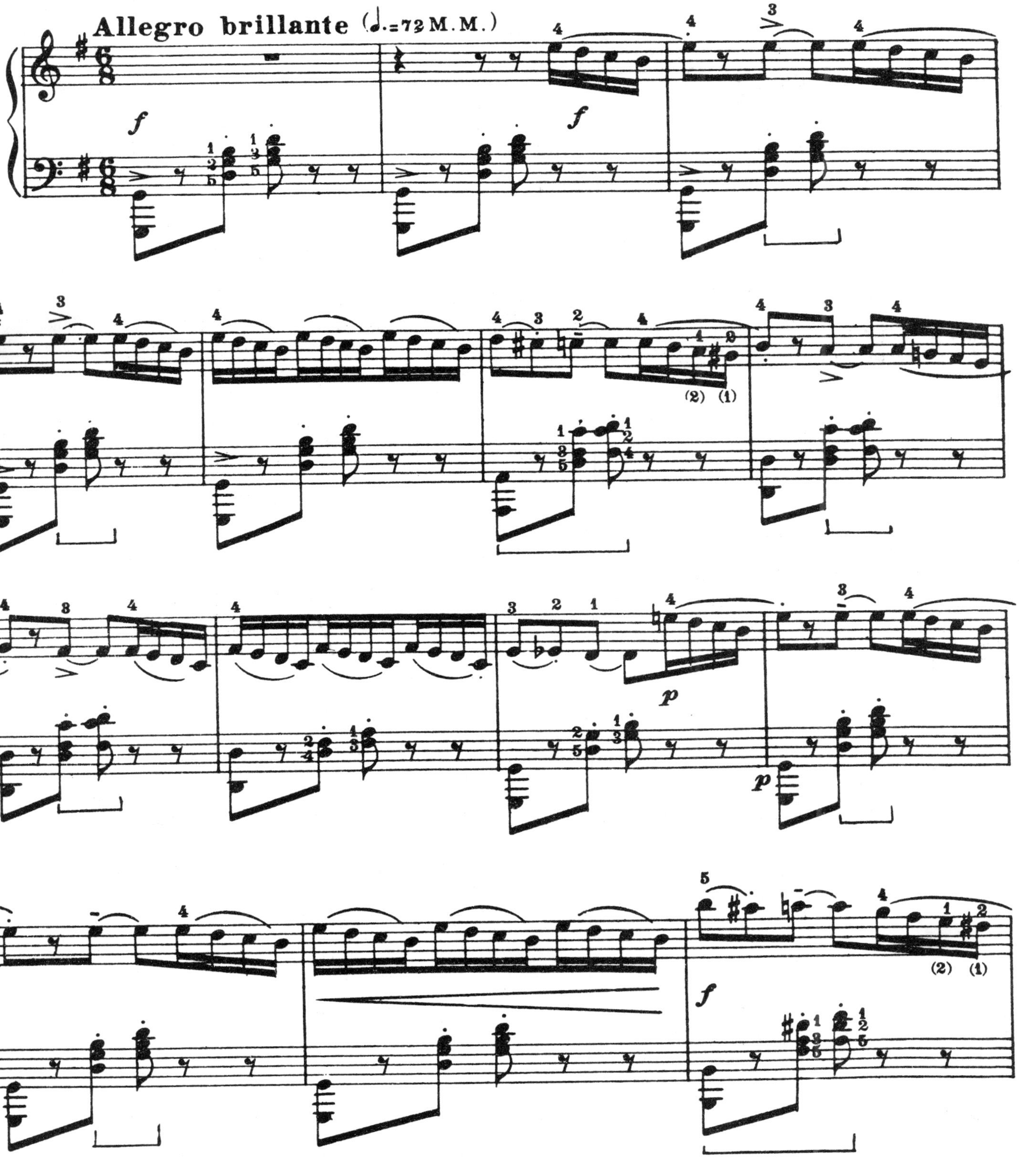

p
f
cresc.
ff
p
p
p
p
f
f
cresc.
ff
p
p
p
pp

pp
f
cresc.
sf
f
p
cresc.
Tempo I
un poco più animato
accelerando poco a poco
ff

(a)
sf
p
pp
f
sf
p
pp
un poco string.
f
8va
8va
ff
ff
(a)
ossia

A Mme. Grant

Valsette

FELIX BOROWSKI
(1872-1956)

cresc.
p
p
dim.
rall.
a tempo
f

l.h.
a tempo
rall.
f
mf
cresc.
Ped. simile

f
dim.
e
rall.
mf
a tempo
f
stringendo
al
fine
ff

★ Humoreske

ANT. DVOŘÁK, Op. 101, No. 7
(1841-1904)

ritard.
f dimin.
pp a tempo
cresc.
ritard.

a tempo
dimin.
dim.

pp

ritard.

a tempo

mf

f

dimin.

p

p

dim.

ritard.

pp dim. ppp

Scotch Poem

From the cragged coast of Scotland
Gazes down an ancient gray castle,
Where the wild breakers dash high.
There, beside the vaulted window,
Stands a fair woman, sweet and frail,
Pale with suff'ring from bitter ills;
And she plays her harp as she sings,
And the wind is tossing her flowing tresses
And bears her mournful song
Over the heaving, boundless sea.

Heinrich Heine

English Version by Alice Mattullath

E. A. MacDOWELL, Op. 31, No. 2
(1861-1908)

Allegro tempestoso

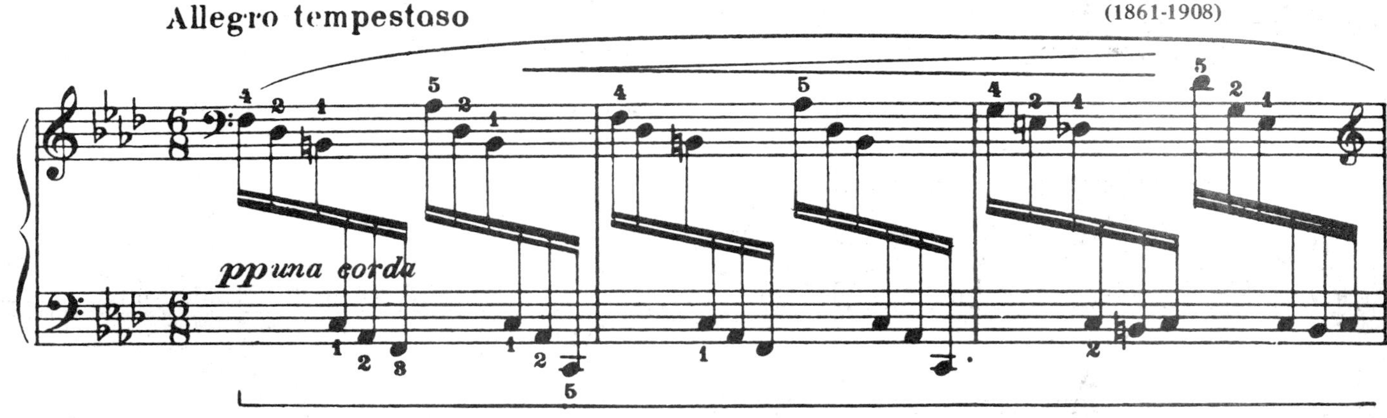

sempre cresc.
fff risouto
cresc.
ff brioso
marcatiss.
poco a poco
dim. e rall.
molto rall.

Andante a piacere
pp parlando ma come di lontano
il basso staccato, quasi arpa
pp
molto rit.
perdendosi
Tempo I
una corda
ppp
tre corde
cresc.
f
sempre cresc.

ff
fff risoluto
brioso
marcatiss.
rall.
molto rall.
Andante
ppp
morendo
una corda

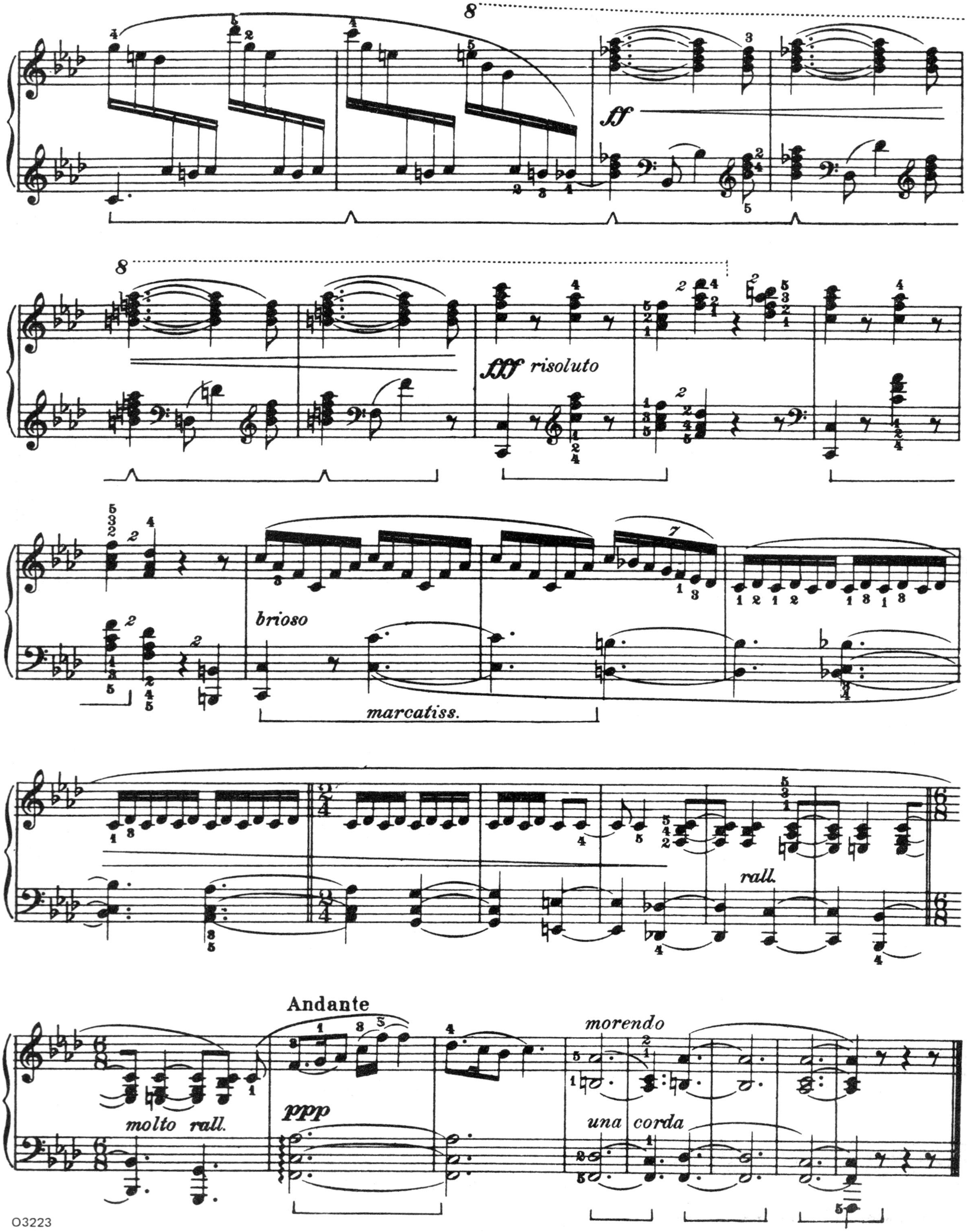

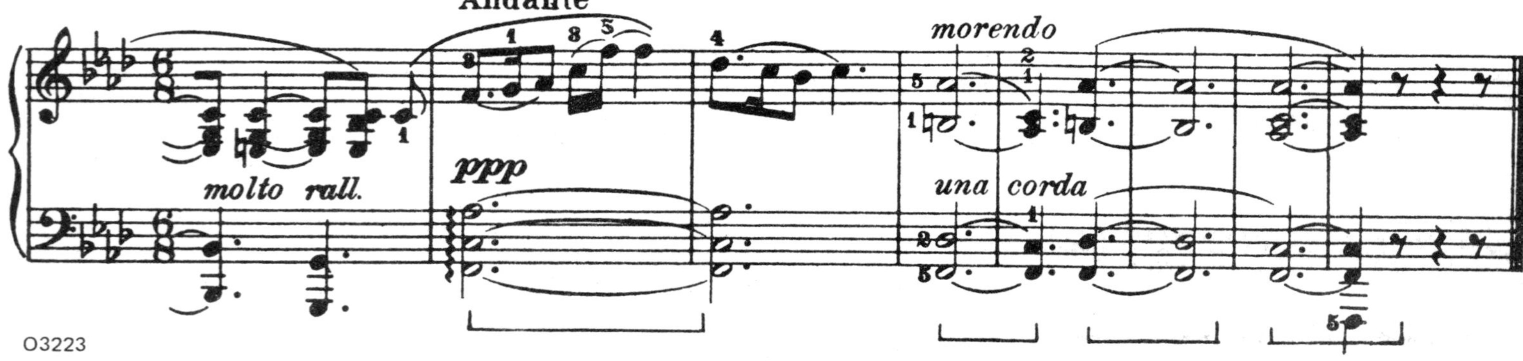

Dance Caprice

Albumleaf

EDVARD GRIEG, Op. 28, No. 3
(1843-1907)

a tempo

f

dim. e rit.

p

poco stretto

a tempo

f

p poco rit.

pp

p

pp

fp

dolcissimo
f
fp
pp
a tempo
poco rit.
p

cres.
p
pp
cres.
f
dim. e poco rit.
a tempo
p
f
p poco rit.
pp

Hungarian Rhapsody No. 2

Themes

FRANZ LISZT (1811-1886)
Arranged by Maxwell Eckstein

*) *Lassan* – Slow movement

dolce con grazia

Friska*

Vivace

pp

*) *Friska* – Quick and spirited movement

rit.
Tempo giusto - Vivace
f marcato
pp

Prestissimo
pp
sempre stacc.
ff
Presto
fz

Austrian Song

J. A. PACHER, Op. 69, No. 1
(1816-1871)

Introduction.
Allegro.

p R. L.

f

p

8

fz

Allegretto.

p

cresc.
f
Cadenza ad lib.
R.H.
L.H.
p

Andante cantabile.
quasi adagio.
pp molto rit.

Allegro.
p
f
A

L.
rit.
a tempo.
L.
cresc.
f
ff

Presto
sempre scherzando

J. HAYDN
(1732-1809)

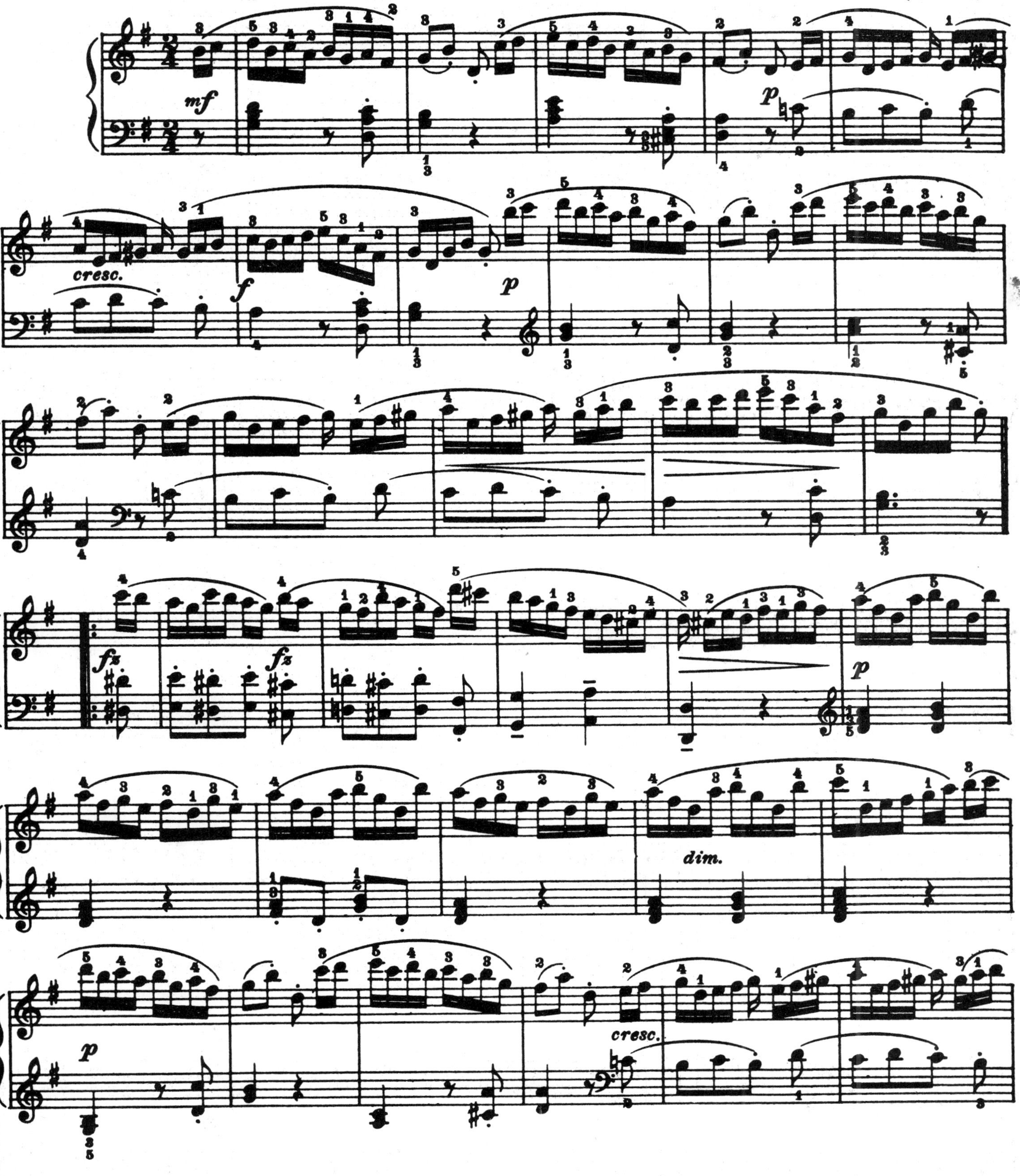

MINORE I

MAGGIORE

MINORE II

f

1. 2.

p

p

cresc.

p

f

p

MAGGIORE

cresc.
fz
fz
f
dim
p
Ped.
Ped.
f
fz
p
p
cresc.
fz
ff

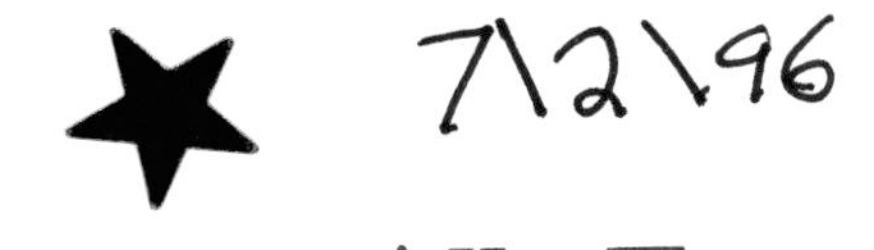

Rondo Alla Turca

FRED. BURGMULLER, Op. 68
(1806-1874)

Allegretto (♩=144)

p

leggiero

sempre stacc. il basso

f

stacc.

p

sf

p

O3223

sf
cresc.
f
dim.
p
sempre stacc.
ff
p
ff
p

p dolce
legato
più f
p
mf
p
p

dim. e poco rit.
sf
p
leggiero
staccato
f
staccato
p

sf
p
sf
cresc.
f
dim.
p
ff
p
ff
p

ben cresc.
stacc.
mf
ff

Valse

AUG. DURAND, Op. 83

mf
f
p e leggiero.
cre
scen
do
f
di
mi
nu
en
do.
p
cre
scen
do
f
di

mi
nu
en
do
p
mf
f
ff
rit.
a tempo.
p
cresc.
ff
ff
Ped. simile
Ped. simile

f
f
p
Ped. simile
cresc.
ff
p

p
poco cresc.
mf
brillante.
cresc.
8va
f
mf
cresc.
poco
a
8va
poco.
f
8va
brillante.
cresc.
ff
f
ff